BASEBALL

BASEBALL

A grand slammin' guide to super baseball!

Mark Crose

A *Sports Illustrated For Kids* Book

First Edition

Library of Congress Cataloging-in-Publication Data

Crose, Mark.
    Make the team. : baseball / Mark Crose. — 1st ed.
        p. cm.
    "A Sports illustrated for kids book."
    Summary: Introduces the history, basic skills and drills, and more complicated plays of baseball.
    ISBN 0-316-16205-1 (hc)
    ISBN 0-316-16207-8 (pb)
    1. Baseball—Juvenile literature. 2. Baseball—History—Juvenile literature. [1. Baseball.] I. Title.
GV867.5.C76 1991
796.357'2—dc20   90-46197

SPORTS ILLUSTRATED FOR KIDS is a trademark of
THE TIME INC. MAGAZINE COMPANY.

Sports Illustrated For Kids Books is a joint imprint of Little, Brown and Company and Warner Juvenile Books. This title is published in arrangement with Cloverdale Press Inc.

10 9 8 7 6 5 4 3 2 1

BP

For further information regarding this title, write to Little, Brown and Company, 34 Beacon Street, Boston, MA 02108

Published simultaneously in Canada by Little, Brown & Company (Canada) Limited

Printed in the United States of America

Interior design by Bernard Springsteel
Interior illustrations by Stanford Kay–Paragraphics

CONTENTS

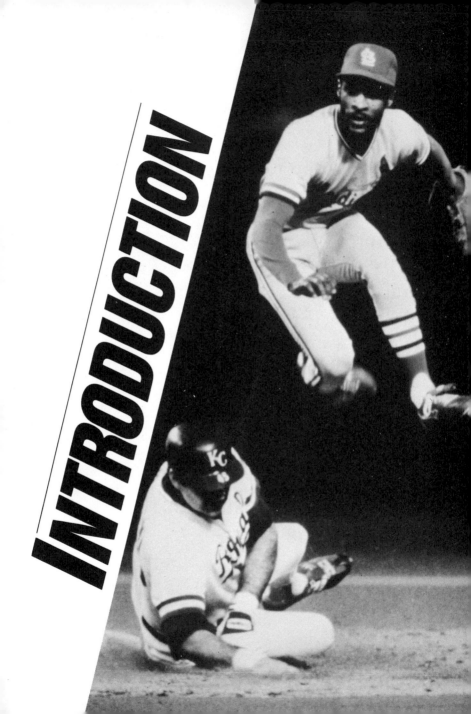

INTRODUCTION

Welcome to the exciting world of baseball! Nothing beats watching a good baseball game. The sound of the bat cracking against the ball at the stadium will always make me lean forward to see how far it's going. When a runner rounds third and heads for home, I know he is going to make it . . . if he is on "my team." Just waiting for my favorite player to come to the plate makes me nervous, hoping that this time he'll hit a home run. The warm sunshine, neatly cut grass and carefully raked dirt around the infield are as inviting to me as a swimming pool on a hot summer day.

No, nothing beats watching a good baseball game. Except playing in one.

This book is for everyone who wants to step out on the field and play. If you don't know anything about how the game is played, turn to the basic summary in the appendix that starts on page 113. This section may also help you understand parts of the game you didn't fully understand before.

The basic skills we will discuss in the rest of the book are designed to do one thing: to let you get more out of baseball. Knowing what to do and how to do it will help you to have more fun with the game.

A Little History

There are many different opinions on who "invented" baseball. The most commonly mentioned name is Abner Doubleday.

Mr. Doubleday was a general in the Civil War. Some baseball historians say that before the war Mr. Doubleday developed most of the rules used in what we now call baseball. This happened back in 1839 in Cooperstown, New York. In honor of Mr. Doubleday's contributions to the game, the Baseball Hall of Fame was built in Cooperstown in 1939.

Other people, though, say that there is no evidence that Mr. Doubleday really invented baseball. Instead, they say, a New York bank clerk named Alexander Cartwright should be given the credit. Mr. Cartwright, they say, laid out the first baseball diamond in 1845 and came up with the basis for our modern rules.

Even before Mr. Doubleday or Mr. Cartwright, there was a game played in England in the 1700s called "rounders." Rounders was played on a diamond-shaped field, just like today's baseball, with bases at the four corners. The batter started at one of the bases and had to hit a pitched ball and run around all the bases in order to score. Three missed swings and the batter was out. Caught fly balls were out as well. It sounds like baseball, doesn't it?

But there was one big difference in rounders. The fielder got the runner out by *hitting him* with the thrown ball.

Can you imagine hitting a dribbler back to a fast pitcher like Nolan Ryan and having him throw the ball at you as you run to first base? Ouch! It's too scary to think about! It is pretty easy to see why they came up with a different rule for baseball.

The game continued to change in America during the late 1800s. The National League of Professional Baseball Clubs was formed in 1876, followed by the American League in 1893. After many years of fighting over which league was better, the two leagues finally agreed in 1903

Who invented baseball? Alexander Cartwright is often credited as being the sport's founder.

to play against each other in a few championship games. The World Series was born!

The All-Star Game is also an important baseball event every year. The tradition started in 1933. The best players from each league come together for an exhibition game that is played in July. Even though the game doesn't count toward anyone's statistics, the natural rivalry between the two leagues makes this game interesting. Nobody wants to be shown up by someone from the other league, so the All-Star players work hard to make sure their team wins.

Legends of the Game

The history of baseball is filled with great players. If you are a big baseball fan, you will want to know more about the following players. Here are the inscriptions from their plaques at the Hall of Fame:

● *Ty Cobb* (played 1905-1928) "Led American League in batting 12 times and created or equaled more major league records than any other player. Retired with 4,191 hits."

● *Cy Young* (played 1890-1911) "Only pitcher in first 100 years of baseball to win 500 games. Among his 511 victories were 3 no-hit shutouts. Pitched perfect game May 5, 1904, allowing no opposing batsman to reach first base."

● *Walter Johnson* (played 1907-1927) "Conceded to be the fastest ball pitcher in history of game. Won 414 games."

● *Christy Mathewson* (played 1900-1916) "Greatest of all the great pitchers in the 20th century's first quarter. Pitched three shutouts in 1905 World Series. First pitcher of the century ever to win 30 games in 3 successive years."

● *George Herman "Babe" Ruth* (played 1915-1935) "Greatest drawing card in history of baseball. Holder of many home run and other batting records. Gathered 714 home runs in addition to 15 in World Series."

● *Henry L. "Lou" Gehrig* (played 1923-1939) "Holder of more than a score of Major and American League records, including that of playing 2,130 consecutive games. When he retired in 1939, he had a lifetime batting average of .340."

As we approach more modern times, we see the names of Joe DiMaggio, Dizzy Dean, Satchel Paige, Roy Cam-

Cy Young was such an incredible pitcher that both the American and National Leagues give an annual pitching award called the Cy Young Award.

panella, Willie Mays, Mickey Mantle, Henry Aaron, Sandy Koufax, Al Kaline, Jim Palmer. . .the list goes on and on. Baseball is rich in history and stars.

Stats Fever!

Baseball fans love statistics—numbers such as home run totals and batting averages. Statistics link the players of the past with the players of today. They make for great debates and endless study.

Open any newspaper during the season and you will find the box scores of games on the sports page. These are almost like a baseball fan's road map. Box scores list all the players who took part in a game and tell how well they pitched, hit and fielded. By looking at the box scores you can see how well every team is playing and compare how each player is performing.

There are many kinds of baseball statistics. You can study a pitcher's ERA (earned run average)—that's how many runs are scored off the pitcher every nine innings, not including runs that score because of errors. You can see the number of RBIs (runs batted in) your favorite player has collected, not to mention his BA (batting average) and HR (home run) totals.

With statistics, it is easy for you to see that Will Clark's batting average today makes him one of the game's greatest hitters. Your grandfather will probably argue that today's pitchers aren't as tough as they used to be, but study the statistics with him!

Your grandfather might tell you that no man since Ted Williams in 1941 has hit over .400 for a season. (Ted batted .406.) But you can point out that Ted wasn't facing relief pitchers as tough as Dennis Eckersley and John Franco.

You can argue until you are blue in the face about who was the toughest pitcher. But nobody can deny the stats on Nolan Ryan. He has over 5,000 strikeouts and five no-hit games. No one else comes close to having statistics as good as that!

It gets tricky when you try to compare players of today with players of the past. The arguments go on forever and will never be resolved. But that is part of the charm of the game. Since baseball has stayed basically the same for so long, it is easy to find the similarities and the differences.

The Basics

But enough about the past! Before we begin talking about the skills you need to play different positions, we should discuss the basics.

It may sound simple, but much of baseball is throwing and catching. Whenever you have a chance, play catch. The first thing you should do is grab a ball and throw it.

Throwing

Hold the ball with the first two fingers of your throwing hand on top of the ball, your thumb underneath, and your last two fingers acting as a brace. With a firm grip, but not too tight, draw your arm back, with your elbow leading the way. Your weight will shift to the leg under your throwing arm, and your shoulders will start turning away from your target. When your elbow won't move back any farther, your shoulders should almost be pointing towards your target in a straight line.

At this point, you're ready to throw. The elbow of your throwing arm should start forward first. This elbow motion will automatically cock your wrist backward and provide a source of power for your throw. Your arm, shoulder and body should flow smoothly toward the target. Your wrist will uncock as you hurl the ball forward.

The ball should feel as though it is rolling off your fingertips as it releases from your hand. Keep smooth, even pressure on the ball.

At all times during this motion, you should be looking directly at your target. Your mind will automatically figure out how far the ball has to go and in what direction, if you let it. Try not to think about anything. Don't consciously aim the ball, just relax and throw.

Accuracy comes from repeated throwing. With practice, it will be a completely automatic response. You will soon pick up a ball, look at your target and throw right to it. *Practice...practice...practice.*

Catching

Catching the ball is the same program as throwing. The more you do it, the easier it becomes. You will be able to see any ball in the air and instantly figure out how far and fast it is coming after you have had enough experience.

The key to catching well is having "soft hands." To understand what that means, picture yourself throwing a ball into a pillow. The ball nestles in softly, doesn't it? But picture the ball hitting a concrete wall instead. It bounces a long way away, right?

You should use your glove like a pillow. Let the ball come into your glove and let your hands "give" slightly. Your hands should move in toward your body. Don't swing your glove out toward the ball or try to grab the ball out of the air. You'll only wind up knocking it away from you.

Hold your hands up right in front of you now. Draw them toward you about an inch or two. That's what your hand action should be as the ball reaches your glove — just a slight give to provide that pillow for the ball to nestle into.

Keep your other hand near the glove. As the ball hits the pocket of your glove, your free hand should be ready to snap over it to prevent the ball from popping out and getting away. This also puts your hand in position to grab the ball quickly out of your glove and throw it back toward your target.

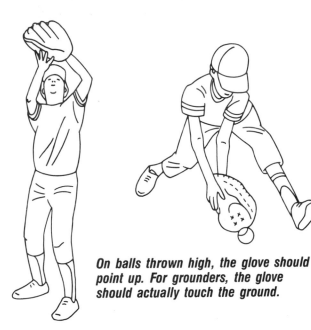

On balls thrown high, the glove should point up. For grounders, the glove should actually touch the ground.

For balls thrown chest high or above, your glove should be fingers up, palm facing the ball. On balls below your wrist, the glove fingers will point down, but keep the palm facing out. For balls that come in between your waist and your chest, you need to have the glove fingers pointing sideways, as if you were catching a Frisbee.

Fielding grounders will be discussed in more detail in later chapters, but here is one basic rule: Get down *low* with your glove touching the ground directly in front of the ball. The fingers of your glove hand should be pointing down, with both hands relaxed and ready to react to whatever bounce the ball takes.

The key is to be relaxed. Simply move your hand toward the ball in a smooth, confident manner. Again, it is experience that makes you a good ball catcher, so get out there and, yes, *practice*.

Chapter 1:

BATTING

Choosing a Bat

The first thing you have to do before you go to the plate is obvious—you have to select a bat. There is no one particular size of bat that is right for all players. Choosing a bat is a matter of personal choice.

Find a bat with the proper weight, handle thickness and balance. Joe DiMaggio, one of the greatest hitters of all time, thought a hitter should use a heavy bat with a thick handle because "the more wood, the more chance he has of hitting the ball." But today's players tend to favor lighter bats, which are easier to control, and can be swung faster. The greater the bat speed, the more powerfully you can hit the ball. A good compromise is to swing the heaviest bat you can comfortably control.

Professionals generally use 34- to 36-inch bats that weigh from 32 to 36 ounces. High school players are in the 32–36 inch area with weights of 30 to 36 ounces. Youth leaguers start at 26 inches and go up to 32 inches. These bats can weigh anywhere from 21 ounces to 32 ounces.

You will learn from swinging different bats what size will work best for you. But start light and find a bat that you can really control. You have to swing the bat. . .don't let the bat swing you!

The Stance

The next thing to do is step into the batter's box and assume your stance. The best stance is the most comfortable one. Your feet should be evenly lined up, about shoulder-width apart with your weight equally distributed. An imaginary bat placed against your toes should

*The correct
batting stance.*

point in a direct line toward the pitcher. If you have trouble
swinging your bat around fast enough, your coach will
help you take either a more "open" or "closed" stance.
"Open" means your front foot (the one closer to the pitcher)
is moved back several inches from the imaginary straight
line. In a "closed" stance, your back foot is dropped back
several inches. This gives you a different angle when you
hit the ball.

Your knees should be bent slightly. Your eyes should
be facing the pitcher and the ball. Here is important rule
number 1: A hitter should move his eyes to follow the
pitched ball. *Never* move the head. Your head will naturally move a little from the force of your swing, but it's
very important to keep your head as still as possible. If

Notice how Lou Gehrig stands in the proper batting stance with his knees slightly bent, his hands close together and his hips and shoulders level.

your head is moving, your swing will be lopsided, and your eyes won't be focused on the ball.

Your hips and shoulders should be kept even. When a player has level hips and shoulders he will make a level swing. It is that simple.

You should grip the bat comfortably. You want to avoid tension and tightness. Your hands should be close together so they can work as a unit. You should start with a firm (but not tight) grip with your bottom hand and a loose grip with your top hand. Your grip tightens naturally during the swing, so this is a good way to start. It also will help you build up power as your bat swings around and makes contact with the ball.

The bat should hit the ball before your wrists start to turn over, or "break." Your swing will naturally bring your top hand over, which makes your wrists roll (breaking) as you finish the swing. Make sure you don't turn your wrists before you hit the ball.

It's this powerful wrist action that can generate tremendous bat speed. When the wrists break just after contact, the swing is given that extra little punch that helps rocket the ball on its way.

Once you have taken your stance and are gripping the bat correctly, you should hold your hands up about chest high. This is called the "ready" position. Having your hands at this height serves two functions. First, you are now in a good position to start your swing. Second, if the ball is coming in higher than your hands, you can tell that it is out of the strike zone.

There have been great hitters in the past who have held their hands much higher than this–players like Carl Yastrzemski, Brooks Robinson, Joe Morgan and many others. But even these players lowered their hands to chest level when they started to swing. It makes sense to simply hold your hands at chest level as soon as you take your stance.

The ready position puts you in the proper stance to begin your swing.

Your Position in the Box

Your position in the batter's box will vary. Experience will make it easier. You should probably start with home plate squarely in front of you as you face either the first base side (if you are righthanded) or third base (if you bat lefthanded).

If you step in to face a fireball pitcher you might want to move your body back a little toward the catcher. This will give you an extra split second to adjust to the speed of his pitches. Sounds easy, doesn't it? But what if someone throws you a curveball? If you are standing at the back end of the batter's box, a curveball will have even more time to curve.

If you are facing a pitcher who throws a lot of "junk" (slower pitches that move around a lot to confuse a hitter), move your body a little ahead of the plate, toward the pitcher. This cuts down the time the pitch has to move around. But beware of the fastball!

Another question is, how close or far away from the plate should you stand? There have been great hitters who crowded the plate, standing almost on top of it. There have been others who stood quite a distance away. I think Ted Williams, one of the all-time greatest hitters, had the right idea. He found that if he crowded the plate, his hands and arms were hanging over it, which made him swing before the ball reached the plate. It was impossible for

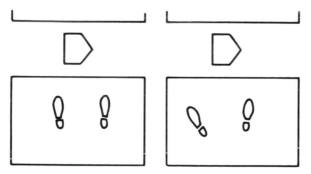

Begin facing either first base (for righthanders) or third base (for lefthanders). You may wish to move back toward the catcher if you're facing a powerful pitcher.

him to hit the ball evenly. If Williams moved away from the plate, about ten inches to a foot, he didn't have to swing so early, especially on inside pitches. "So don't crowd the plate," Williams told people. "Turn toward the pitcher with your front shoulder and step toward him so that your momentum and weight are going right back toward him. This enables you to keep your head down so that you are looking at the pitch all the time."

Since this is advice from a man who hit more than 500 home runs and who had a career batting average above .300, I think you should listen to it carefully. Again, every batter will find the style that is the most comfortable for him. But start out with some smart basics by listening to the great hitters.

The Strike Zone

A pitch that crosses home plate anywhere between your knees and armpits is a strike. When you are batting, you want to swing only at strikes. If you swing at pitches that are out of the "strike zone," you'll probably either miss the ball or not hit it very well.

Reggie Jackson, a tremendous home run hitter who helped the Oakland A's and the New York Yankees win the World Series, knows how important it is to swing only at strikes. He once said, "When you start hitting at balls that are two or three inches inside or outside [the strike zone], or high or low, you're giving the pitcher a bigger strike zone to shoot for. This means you'll see fewer good pitches to hit. Know the strike zone and make that pitcher throw where you want it."

Reggie blasted 540 homers in his career. He also holds

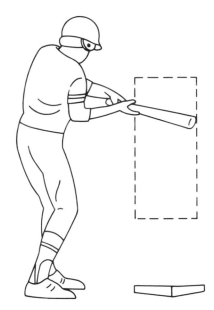

The strike zone.

the record for being struck out the most, so he knows from experience what he is talking about.

In other words, a good hitter must be patient. Don't swing at everything that is thrown your way. Wait until you get the pitch you want, then rip into it.

Also, don't watch the body motion of the pitcher. Just focus on the ball as it leaves his hand, and follow it all the way to either your bat or the catcher's glove.

The Swing

If you were to watch films of all the batting champions over the years, one thing would stand out. They all have smooth, natural, *level* swings. By simply trying to make solid contact with the ball, they hit more line drives and have fewer strikeouts than players who try to *kill* the ball when they hit it.

When you make contact with the ball, you always have a chance to get a hit. But when you swing for the fences and end up hitting nothing, you take a lot of long walks back to the dugout after striking out.

Stepping toward the ball as you swing gives you power. Try to swing a bat a few times while you are standing flat-footed. You'll find it's hard to keep your balance. You aren't able to swing the bat very quickly. Now take your stance and try this instead: As you imagine the pitch coming in, shift your weight slightly backward to start your swing motion. With your weight back, lift your front foot and step toward the pitcher as you swing. Your swing should feel stronger and faster. And your balance should be much better as well.

On a low pitch, the hitter must bend his knees a little more as he steps. That way, his whole body is lower and his bat will be more level with the ball.

I remember a horrible batting slump I was in once. I couldn't get a hit no matter how hard I tried. After a couple of games, I could barely make contact. I had no idea what was wrong. Luckily my coach, who knew my swing pretty well, stopped me after I had hit another weak grounder. "Keep that front shoulder in there, kid. You're pulling out."

A light bulb turned on in my head.

The front shoulder is a very important part of your swing. I was moving mine away from the ball too soon. This caused my body to turn slightly. Instead of hitting the ball on the fat part of the bat, I was making contact at the end. That led to some pretty wimpy hits.

The coach told me to tuck my chin in close to my front shoulder. That helped me keep it from pulling out. Of course, your shoulder will pull out and away as you complete your swing, but this should happen only *after* you make contact.

So what have we talked about so far?

1) Select a bat you can control comfortably.

2) Take a balanced stance, with your feet directly under your shoulders.

3) Hold your hands up, about chest high.

4) Keep your eyes focused on the ball at all times.

5) Step toward the pitcher as you make a smooth, level swing at the ball right in front of the plate.

6) Follow all the way through on the swing, until your arms are fully extended.

Mike Schmidt, the Philadelphia Phillies' all-time great third baseman and one of the top home run hitters of all time, once said, "It's not just one part of the swing that enables the batter to hit the ball with authority. It's everything! You have to put everything together—the shoulders, arms, hips, wrists and hands."

That is the secret: All parts of the swing must work together. Smooth timing is the key to good hitting!

It Takes Guts!

To be a truly good hitter, you must also have courage. The first few times you step up to the plate, it's natural to worry about getting hit. There will be balls that come humming in right toward you. But try not to worry about it. After all, if you were playing dodgeball with friends, would you worry about someone trying to hit you from 45 or 60 feet away? Probably not. In dodgeball, you're relaxed and ready to move in any direction to get away.

It should be the same when you're standing at the plate.

You have time to get away from a bad pitch if you need to. What I recommend is a very simple and safe trick: When you see a pitch that looks like it is coming straight at you, just roll your front shoulder in toward your body. Step away from the plate as you do this, and you're home free. If the pitch hits you, it will bounce off your shoulder, hip or even the back of your helmet. No problem.

The important thing is, *don't panic.* If you freeze in the batter's box and let a pitch hit you in the front half of your body, you might get hurt. Remember to turn away from the pitcher, so your back is facing the pitcher's mound. When you have confidence standing up at bat, you will become a more aggressive hitter. And a more aggressive hitter is a better hitter.

Switch-hitting

If you are strong, coordinated and confident in your swing, you might think about giving switch-hitting a try. Switch-hitting is when you bat from the left side of the plate when there's a righthanded pitcher, and from the right side when there's a lefthanded pitcher.

The main advantage to switch-hitting is that you will always see the pitch coming toward you. If the pitcher throws a curveball, for example, it will curve toward you. This makes it easier to see and react to.

I am righthanded, and sometimes pitched sidearm. This usually scared righthanded batters, who thought that my pitches were coming right at them. It was hard for them to stay in the box and take a good swing. But a switch-hitter will never have that problem. There is

It takes courage and confidence to be a good hitter. Even power hitters like Jose Canseco had to start somewhere.

29

another slight advantage as well. A lefthanded batter stands about a step and a half closer to first base. On a ground ball in the infield, that split second might make the difference between being out or safe.

Switch-hitting requires a great deal of coordination, timing and ambidexterity (being able to use both hands well). It is not easy for everyone. Try it a few times when you're practicing. It will take a lot of work, but it might prove useful for you. Mickey Mantle, Howard Johnson and Willie McGee learned how to switch-hit for their baseball careers.

Joe DiMaggio slides his hand up the bat as he squares off for a bunt.

Bunting

Now that we've talked about how to make a good full swing, I'm going to throw a change-up to you. It's time to learn about bunting.

There are three types of bunts we need to talk about: sacrifice bunts, suicide squeezes and bunting for a base hit. All of them can be extremely important. A successful bunt is often the difference between winning and losing a close ball game.

Just the threat of a bunt can help. If the opposing

A successful bunt can make all the difference in a close game.

infielders are worried you might bunt, it brings them closer to home plate. Then it's easier for you to swing away and hit a ground ball between them for a hit.

There are several different techniques to laying down a good bunt. Most coaches agree that younger players should start out by squaring their body toward the pitcher's mound. You do this by moving your front foot back and your back foot forward, so you are facing the pitcher. Bend your knees a little. From this position, slide your top hand up the bat so your hands are a few feet apart. Grip the bat firmly with both hands, but not tightly.

The proper technique for squaring off for a bunt.

Hold the bat up high, at the top of the strike zone (which is just below your armpits, right?). Before you make contact with the ball, lower the bat so it is at the same height as the ball. By moving the bat down, rather than up, you can generally keep yourself from hitting a pop-up, which is the death of a bunt.

The direction the ball goes depends on the angle of the bat. In other words, if your bat is facing third base, the ball will naturally go in that direction.

You want the ball to hit the fat end of the bat. Don't jab the bat at the ball. Just let the bat "deaden" the ball,

as if you are simply blocking the ball. In a good bunt, the ball will roll to the halfway point between the catcher and pitcher, either toward the third base or first base side.

If there is a runner on second base, you want to bunt toward third base. This forces the third baseman to come forward to get the ball, so the shortstop has to run over and cover third. If you have a runner on first, bunt toward the first baseman. It takes him away from the base and forces all the other infielders to rotate around. This gives the runner a better chance to get to the next base safely. Usually the hitter who bunts will be thrown out at first base, which is why this play is called a sacrifice bunt.

Normally, a sacrifice bunt is not used unless the score is close, there is a runner on first or second base, and there are fewer than two outs. Remember that on a sacrifice bunt you shouldn't try to bunt the ball unless the pitch is a strike.

On a suicide squeeze, you *have* to bunt the ball no matter where it is pitched. That's one reason why the suicide squeeze is one of baseball's most exciting plays. The runner on third races toward the plate as soon as the pitcher releases the ball. The batter must get a piece of the pitch and lay down a bunt. Since the runner is already headed toward home, he should be able to score easily if the bunt is correctly executed. If the hitter misses the bunt, however, the catcher will have the ball in his glove and will be able to tag out the runner.

There is a third type of bunt: The bunt for a hit. The secret to success on this play is to not let the other team know what you are going to do. You must wait until the last possible second to square around to bunt. If you move too soon, the infielders will be tipped off and will charge into position. But if you pull it off just right, you can catch a third baseman or first baseman off guard and beat the ball to first base. The bunted ball can either be pushed toward third or dragged down the first base line.

Summary

When it comes to batting, remember the following important points:

- Know the strike zone and only swing at strikes.
- Make sure your step toward the pitcher is smooth.
- Hit the ball where it is pitched. This is called "going with the pitch."
- Maintain a level swing. It's your best chance for solid contact.
- Keep the front shoulder in, until your follow-through lifts it naturally.
- Watch the ball every instant after it leaves the pitcher's hand.
- Be confident that you can hit any pitch.
- Practice. . .practice. . .and practice some more!

Chapter 2:

PITCHING

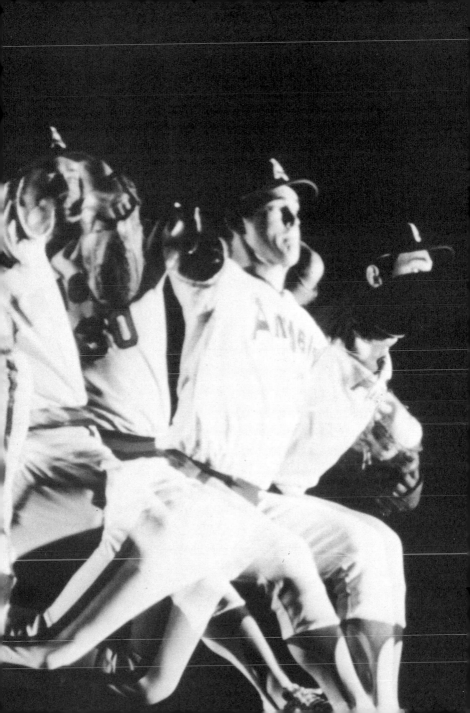

*T*he basic struggle in baseball is pitcher versus batter. Whenever I took the mound, it was "me against them"...until the ball went bouncing past me toward the infield. Then I realized what a team game baseball really is. But even now, I always feel for the pitchers when I watch a game. If you try it, you'll know what I mean.

The Fundamentals

There are three basic skills a pitcher needs in order to be effective. She has to be able to throw hard. She needs to be able to make the ball move. And she needs control. The most important skill is to be able to control the ball. In fact, the second most important skill is control. And so is the third! A pitcher must be able to put the ball *exactly* where she wants it, every time, in order to succeed.

Throwing hard is very important, too, of course. A good fastball pitcher can throw the ball past a lot of hitters. Unfortunately, you can't teach an arm to be strong. That is why coaches and scouts are always looking for someone who can throw bullets naturally.

But power alone is not enough, either. Good hitters can keep up with fast pitchers. I remember a classic battle in an American League playoff game in the 1970s. Goose Gossage of the New York Yankees, the hardest-throwing relief pitcher in baseball at the time, took the mound to face George Brett of the Kansas City Royals. George is a career .330 hitter and once hit nearly .400 in a season.

Goose came in as pitcher late in a very close game. He decided to try to blow his hardest fastball past George. *Whoosh! Pow!* George swung and blasted it deep over the rightfield wall for a home run and a K.C. victory. So you see, speed alone isn't enough.

The ability to make the ball move is what keeps a batter off balance. If a great hitter like George knows you're coming in with a fastball, he will be ready to hit it. But if you can mix up your pitches, throw change-ups and breaking balls, the batter will never know what to expect.

Is It Okay to Throw Breaking Balls?

There has been a lot of discussion, research and argument about whether it is safe for young pitchers to throw breaking (curving) balls. When you're young, your arm is still developing. Throwing breaking balls puts a lot of strain on your arm. If you throw too many too soon, you could permanently hurt yourself.

In the first few years of pitching, when you are 7 to 10 years old, throwing the ball over the plate is your main goal. You shouldn't try to be a pitching wizard yet. But as you develop, and the batters you face improve, you will want to work on throwing a simple curveball.

I'll talk about the basic curve in this chapter. You and your parents should talk about if and when you should start throwing it. Remember, it's more important to have a good, lively arm and control when you start pitching than it is to have a good curve.

39

The Grip

When you grab a baseball and get ready to throw, the natural tendency is to hold it between your thumb and the first two fingers. This is another example of "natural is best." *Do it!*

It's important to remember to hold the ball as far out on the end of your fingers and thumb as you can without losing control of the ball. You don't want to choke the ball. Just have a firm, comfortable grip.

You will grip the ball either across the seams or with the seams. A fastball thrown *with* the seams will usually sink. A fastball thrown *across* the seams will rise. Since you throw these pitches with the same motion, it will be very hard for the batter to know which way the ball is going to move.

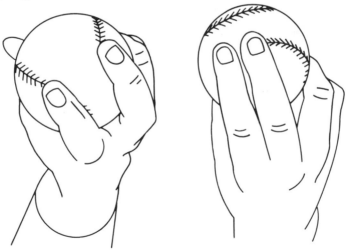

Gripping a fastball with the seams causes the ball to sink. Holding it across the seams allows the ball to rise.

What makes the ball move, in a fastball or a curve, is spin. Roger Craig, coach of the San Francisco Giants, was a major league pitcher in his playing days. He says that the basic idea in pitching is to "get the ball to spin in the direction you want, then apply more spin or speed to make it move as much as you want. To do this you need a combination of loose, fast wrist and finger action."

To understand this better, throw some balls and try to feel the ball rolling off your fingertips. Then put your thumb in a slightly different position and see what happens.

The Delivery

In order to throw good pitches, you need to develop a comfortable delivery. Every pitcher seems to have a slightly different way of throwing the ball, but all of them do two things: They swing their whole arm smoothly, and they follow that with a powerful wrist snap. Any half-armed, jerky motions will put too much stress on the elbow and will eventually ruin your pitching arm.

There are four basic deliveries: overhand, three-quarters, sidearm and underhand. Most pitchers throw with a three-quarters or overhand delivery. Again, however you throw the ball naturally is probably the best way for you. That way will probably be a three-quarters delivery, which refers to the angle of your arm when you throw. An overhand delivery means your arm swings straight around, passing by your ear. A sidearm whips the ball from your side, almost at hip level. A three-quarters throw is midway between the two.

No matter what delivery is used, a pitcher must have

Sandy Koufax throws an overhand shot.

balance, a proper pivot, correct stride and good follow-through. We'll discuss all these shortly. Practice will give you the coordination and rhythm needed to combine all these into an effective delivery.

After "discovering" your style of delivering the ball, you need to work on your pre-pitch routine. Standing on the mound, you should keep the ball hidden from the hitter's view. Hide the pitching hand and the ball behind your back or in your glove. The less the hitter sees the ball, the harder it is for her to find it and hit it.

Most pitchers stand with their pivot foot—the foot that your body turns on—on the pitching rubber. The toes of your pivot foot should be just over the front of the rubber. The other foot should be a few inches behind the rubber and just to the left.

Keep your weight on the back foot. It is easier to turn and throw to another base if your weight is on the back foot. Exactly where your foot should be on the rubber depends on where the batter is standing and the type of pitch you want to throw. By moving your foot to one side of the rubber, you change the angle that the ball will cross the plate. But this is something to think about only after you have learned to control the ball.

In the windup, your body weight moves backward and then forward. This gives your pitch power and speed.

Most pitchers start the windup by stepping back on their non-pivot foot. At the same time, the arms swing down and back. With the weight pulled back, the pitcher is ready to throw the ball with all the power she can. If you've ever fired a bow, you know that the farther you pull the string back, the faster the arrow soars.

Don Newcombe pitching sidearm.

Dan Quisenberry pitching side-arm.

A proper pivot is very important. Your weight will be on your rear foot as your arm comes up over your head during the windup. As your weight starts to move forward again, your front foot should turn (pivot) on the rubber, so the toe almost faces third base (first base if you pitch lefthanded). This motion helps to get your hips pointed in the right direction. Watch a pitcher's belt line. A fast pitcher will be tilted at the hips during her windup.

The leg kick happens naturally. The knee of your non-pivot foot should come up across the body as the arms swing down and back. This helps to bend the body backward so that, again, the entire body will fire the ball forward, like an arrow.

The next movement in a pitch is thrusting forward. As we've just discussed, your back leg will bend, which lowers your whole body. The lower you are, the easier it is to push off the rubber. Tom Seaver did this really well. He dropped his body so low, before driving the ball forward, that his knee got dirty from scraping the ground.

When your back foot is planted firmly in the dirt again, before you reach the top point of your delivery, it should be facing straight toward the plate. This will give you better control as you direct your pitch.

The muscles in your arm should not be tense, or you won't have a smooth delivery. Your hand and wrist should be relaxed also, so that you can give the ball a strong snap with the wrist.

Finally, after throwing the ball, keep your arm flowing smoothly until it wraps around your body. This is called "follow-through," and helps keep you from giving the ball the wrong spin.

This all sounds pretty difficult, doesn't it? But with

The pre-pitch routine.

practice, it will all happen naturally. Then you can remember one more thing: Keep your eye on the target! During each step on the mound, keep your attention focused on what you are trying to do. Don't let anything distract you.

Types of Pitchers

The next thing to consider is when to throw what pitch. By changing your grip on the ball, and the amount and type of wrist action you use, you can throw three basic pitches and several specialty pitches.

The basic pitches are fastballs, curveballs, and change-ups. The specialty pitches are sinkers, sliders, screwballs, forkballs, knuckleballs, and split-finger fastballs. I'll only discuss the fastball, curveball and change-up here. The other pitches are more advanced, and should be learned later in your baseball career.

The Fastball

We've talked a little about the fastball already. There is no "best" way to throw it. You just rear back and fire. Remember to keep your delivery smooth and use strong wrist and forearm action. You should never try to throw the ball as hard as you can. Everything in your body would tighten up, which could injure your arm. If you speed up your pitch smoothly, you will develop a truly fast fastball.

The Curve

There are many ways to grip the ball for a curve, but most pitchers hold the ball at the point where the seams come together. The first two fingers are close together and

The pitcher's leg kick.

the thumb is stretched out. Remember to grip the ball along the length of the seams to make the ball sink. Grip it across the seams to get it to rise.

In the windup, your wrist should be cocked backward when your arm is close to the rear of your head. When your elbow starts forward toward the plate, the wrist turns over and snaps downward, putting a lot of spin on the ball. The ball should roll smoothly, over the first and second joints of the first finger, like a ball rolling off a table.

The longer you can wait to release the ball the better. Pretend you are trying to tickle your ear when you throw a curveball. This will help keep your wrist tucked in correctly. When you are ready to throw the ball, really snap the wrist as hard as you can. That is how you give the ball its spin.

Keep curveballs low. A curve thrown high will usually "hang" in the air at the batter's eye level, making it easy for him to hit. There have been more hanging curves sent into orbit than any other pitch.

It takes a lot of practice to get the spin just right. But this pitch strains your arm, so don't overdo it. And make sure you, your parents, and your coach all agree that it is safe for you to learn it.

The Change-Up

The change-up is a slow pitch that comes after a fastball, to catch the batter off guard. It should be thrown with a stiff wrist, just like pulling down a window shade. The bottom part, or heel, of the hand comes down first. The ball slides up your hand and rolls off your fingertips.

Another popular method of throwing a change-up is to stuff the ball back in the palm of your hand. Then just throw it, using very little wrist action.

This pitch is designed to throw the batter's timing off. Your windup will look just like you are throwing a fastball, but it will take longer for the ball to get to the plate because you aren't giving it any wrist action.

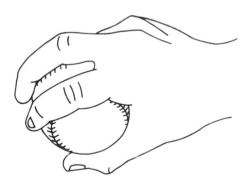

*The correct grip
for the curveball.*

Summary

- Be consistent in your windup.
- Keep the ball hidden from the batter throughout your delivery.
- Make a good pivot, turning your front foot until it is almost parallel to the rubber.
- Use your hips properly.
- Have a well-balanced leg lift.
- Keep your eyes fixed on the target.
- Drive off the rubber with a powerful thrust, right toward the hitter.
- Use a smooth arm motion, including strong wrist action.
- Follow through smoothly.
- THROW STRIKES!

Fielding As a Pitcher

The pitcher, besides delivering the ball to the plate, acts as the fifth infielder. Handling batted balls, throwing accurately to the bases, covering and backing up bases and providing field leadership are some of the things pitchers need to do.

We discussed your follow-through earlier. A smooth, balanced delivery and follow-through should leave you in a perfect fielding position. The instant after the ball leaves your hand, you should be ready for action. You might need to field a sharply hit ball up the middle, turn, throw to a base, and then run and back up another base.

On any bunt or slow grounder, the pitcher should hurry to field the ball. This frees your infielders to cover their bases. Try to get in front of the ball, keep your eyes on it all the way into your glove and then throw accurately to the proper base.

What base you throw to depends on the situation. With nobody on a base, you would obviously throw to first. With runners on base, ideally you would try to get the lead runner (the one closest to home) out. This requires a snap decision after you pick up the ball. A quick glance is all you will have time for.

On any bunt or slow grounder hit to your left, you should run for first base right away. Many games have been lost because the pitcher forgot this simple rule. The first baseman will usually run for the bunted ball. So you should dash toward first, keeping yor eyes on the bag until you get within about 15 feet. When you know you are headed correctly toward the base, turn and watch for the throw from the first baseman as you run. Watch the ball until it lands in your glove, then turn and find the bag. Step on the infield side of the bag to keep yourself from crashing into the runner.

You will also have to cover home plate sometimes. If there is a runner on third (or a fast one at second) and the ball gets past your catcher, you must race toward the plate as fast as you can and cover home. Kneel at the inside half of the plate when you are facing the right direction for the throw. You don't want to block the plate by standing on the outside half because the runner could crash into you. Make sure the ball is held tightly inside your glove.

Every ball that is hit into the outfield is a backup play for the pitcher. Once you decide which base the ball is going to be thrown to, race to a position 20 or 30 feet behind the bag. You should be lined up with the outfielder who is throwing. If the ball is thrown badly or gets past the baseman, you'll be there to stop it.

Chapter 3:

CATCHING

"The Field General." That's the catcher. Every catcher I've known has been a take-charge sort of guy. He directs the play of his team, handles his pitchers, keeps the runners honest (so they don't steal bases), and keeps the whole team alert. In short, he runs the game. Every team needs a skilled, clever and highly spirited catcher. The confidence of the pitcher and the entire defense rests on him.

Besides having a strong arm, and strong legs, the catcher must be smart. He must also be able to talk easily to his teammates, especially the pitcher. The catcher needs to make the pitcher think he can strike any batter out. And if the catcher thinks his pitcher is running out of gas, he has to let the coach know.

The Equipment

The catcher's glove is different than any other player's. It is a large circular mitt with lots of padding and a very deep pocket. The padding comes in handy when your pitcher is zipping fastballs at you.

The catcher should also wear hard plastic shin guards, a foam-filled chest protector, a face mask and a helmet. The catcher will be hit by a lot of foul balls and bad pitches, so he needs all this gear to protect him.

With all of this equipment, the catcher is safe, but he is also heavy. Standing, kneeling, running and throwing with all that added weight can be tough. That's why catchers must work hard to be in top shape.

The Catcher's Stance and Signals

When you crouch down waiting for a pitch, you must be well balanced so you can react quickly. You need to be able to move toward the pitch or jump up to field a bunt or throw out a runner trying to steal a base. Your hands and arms should be relaxed but ready for action.

The most important thing to remember is to give your pitcher a good target with your mitt. Hold your hand so the entire open pocket of the mitt is facing your pitcher. The bigger the target area, the easier it is for the pitcher to relax and aim.

There are many ideas on where to hold your bare hand while waiting for the pitch. Catchers used to curl up their fingers and tuck the hand behind the mitt. That way the bare hand was close enough to fish the ball out of the glove fast.

But in the last few years, virtually everyone has gone to a one-handed catching style. The famous Cincinnati Reds catcher Johnny Bench made it popular during his career in the 1970s. He kept his bare hand tucked behind his back until the ball got past the hitter.

The reason for this is pretty obvious if you've ever been hit on your bare hand by a foul ball. A lot of major league catchers used to miss games because they had broken fingers. With the hand held behind the back, there are fewer injuries.

We won't spend a lot of time in this book talking about signals between the catcher and pitcher. Later in your baseball career, you will want to study it more. The catcher and pitcher must both know where the pitch is going to

*The catcher signals
the pitcher to throw
a curveball.*

go. For example, if a catcher is positioned on the inside corner of the plate and is expecting a fastball, he will never be able to catch a curveball that is breaking away on the outside corner of the plate.

Signals are usually flashed by the fingers. One finger is a fastball, two is a curve, three is a slider, and so on. You can also signal whether the pitch should be high or low, inside or outside. You might use different signals when a runner is on base and might be able to see the signals and warn the batter. Your coach will discuss signals in more detail with you when the time is right.

Positioning

All great catchers find a way to move as close as possible to the hitter. Don't get so close that the bat can hit your mitt (or your head!), but work your way forward slowly until you find the right spot.

There are many reasons for this. It is easier to catch the pitch if you are closer to the strike zone. You will be able to get to bunts faster. Foul tips are easier to grab because they have less room to move. And you will be able to handle low pitches easier.

That last point is important. If there are runners on base, especially on third, it is crucial that you block low throws and keep them from getting behind you.

When a pitch is coming in and you know it's going to be low, you must react right away. If it's coming in straight, drop to the ground on your knees and form a wall with your body. This will keep the ball from bouncing between your legs and hitting the backstop behind you.

If the pitch is either left or right of the plate, drop the knee on the side of the pitch and slide your whole body over in front of it. If you can't get your glove on it, you hope that the ball will hit the soft part of your body. This prevents the ball from bouncing far away.

On a low pitch, turn your glove so your palm is facing up. This allows you to use the glove like a shovel, and you can "dig" the ball out of the dirt. If the ball hits the ground far in front of the plate and bounces up high, you still might have time to whip your glove up and catch it. If not, your chest protector should stop it.

Throwing

A catcher needs to know how to throw three different ways: a full overhand throw, a snap throw and a side-arm toss.

Your footwork as a catcher will determine how well you throw. If you shift your weight properly, you will have the rhythm, power and quickness that you need.

Block low balls with your whole body by dropping to the ground.

If you are a righthanded catcher and need to throw overhand to second base, shift your weight to the right foot. Rotate your shoulders to the right while the ball is swung over the right shoulder. Try to grip the ball across the seams so the ball will have the necessary backspin to make the ball go straight and sink slightly just in front of your target. Cock your arm just behind your ear and throw as quickly as you can, releasing the ball with a sharp wrist and arm snap while pushing off your right foot.

The snap throw is similar, except the arm is not pulled back as far. This is a short, quick motion used on throws to first or third base.

The sidearm flip is used when you are fielding bunts quickly, and don't have time to straighten up to throw overhand.

Proper footwork is essential for a catcher to throw well.

The Pop Fly

Anything hit in fair territory is best left to an infielder coming in on the play. But foul pops behind the plate are the catcher's job.

If a foul ball is hit over your left shoulder, you should naturally turn to your left and start searching the sky for it. If it is over your right shoulder, turn to your right. Since it is difficult to see through your mask, you should slip it off and hold it in your bare hand until you locate the pop-up. Once you know where the ball is and how to get to it, throw the catcher's mask away from the play so you won't step on it.

When a ball is popped up behind the plate, it has a tremendous amount of spin on it. This spin makes the ball move just like a curveball thrown by a pitcher. Because of this spin, pop fouls have an "infield drift,"

The catcher is responsible for catching foul pops. Here, Yogi Berra lunges to catch the ball. He keeps his hands in front of him in order to cradle the ball.

meaning the ball will tend to drift back toward the infield. The higher the pop, the more drift it will have. This is why most catchers like to catch pop-ups with their back toward the infield.

Try to keep the ball in front of you, stepping back enough to allow for its drift. Once you have spotted it, get your hands up right away so you are ready to make the catch.

Most catchers will catch pop-ups like an outfielder catches a fly—with their glove held over the head. The glove can shield your eyes from the sun and your bare hand can slip over the ball when it goes into the mitt.

But some successful catchers catch the ball in front of their stomachs. They can cradle the ball softly in their glove this way. Or, if the ball hits their glove and bounces, they have a second chance to lunge for it before it hits the ground.

Whichever method you prefer, what comes *naturally* should be the one you use. Either way, the key is to practice. You will need to see a lot of pop-ups before you get comfortable under them and know what to do.

Johnny Bench once said that he could tell by the sound of the ball coming off the bat if it was going to be a ball he could make a play on. Now that's experience!

Fielding Bunts

As soon as you see a batter square around to bunt, your whole body should go on alert. All bunts should be fielded with two hands. Put the glove in front of the ball and scoop the ball into it with your throwing hand. Do this in one motion and *never* take your eyes off the ball!

When a ball is bunted down the third base line, there are two different ways to handle it. Most catchers turn their backs to first base and run to the ball as quickly as they can. This is the fastest way.

But many catchers like to circle around the ball so they can keep the play in front of them while they throw to first. If you circle the ball, you just pick it up, step and throw. With the other method, you have to grab the ball, spin around and then throw.

The catcher is the only one able to see the entire field. If you see a chance to tag a scoring runner out,

The Rundown

There will be times when a runner on third base gets caught between third and home. This is a rundown. The catcher's jog is very simple. When the ball comes to you, run the base runner back toward third. As soon as the third baseman is ready, make an accurate, chest-high throw to him so he can tag the runner.

After you toss the ball, move back toward home in case

let your teammates know to throw the ball directly to you.

something goes wrong at third. You and your third baseman should both work on the infield side of the line when you throw. This way the runner won't be blocking your vision and you won't have to throw "through" him. One throw should be all that is needed in a proper rundown. *Don't* let your third baseman chase the runner toward you. Always chase the runner back toward the base from which he is coming!

Other Fielding Tips

One of your other jobs as a catcher is to cover bases. When a ground ball is hit to the infielders and there are no runners on base, you should move quickly down the first base line in foul territory so you can back up the first baseman.

On throws to home plate from the outfield, remember that only you can see the whole field. If you have a chance to tag out the runner trying to score, and the throw looks good, yell out that the ball should go directly to you. Don't let a "cutoff man" catch it midway.

If you can see that the throw is wide or that the runner will beat it, yell out "cutoff!" or just "cut!" If the ball isn't wasted by throwing it home, you can keep other baserunners from getting extra bases.

Summary

- Be a field general and direct the play of your fielders on all batted balls.
- Talk to your pitcher. Calm him down when neces-

sary, and pump him up when he needs it.

- Keep pop-ups in front of you and let the infielders handle all that they can.

- Back up first base on all batted balls when the bases are empty. Otherwise you need to stay home and guard the plate.

- Talk to your cutoff men so they know whether to let the ball go in to the plate or not.

- Control bad pitches by keeping the ball in front of you.

- Give your pitcher a good target!

Remember that no one can learn everything about catching overnight. It takes a lot of practice and experience. The more time you spend behind the plate, the better. Even when you're not on the field, study other good catchers. Watch how they set up and move behind the plate. During batting practice or out in the bullpen, work on the proper habits. Don't be lazy.

Chapter 4:

INFIELD

You want action? Get ready. In the infield you will get *lots* of action.

First Base

A first baseman who is good with his glove can prevent more runs from scoring for the other team than he could ever drive in as a batter. . .believe me!

If you are good at going up in the air for high throws or scooping low throws out of the dirt, you will make your teammates more confident. And the better you are at those plays, the fewer you will have to make. Everyone will throw more accurately to you if they are confident.

A first baseman needs good hands, a strong arm, coordination, quickness and intelligence. It helps if you are tall, too! Many coaches like to use left handed first basemen. A left handed player at that position has an easier time on double plays. He can catch the ball and throw to second without having to turn his body like a righthander does. If you can also hit the ball as well as New York Yankees first baseman Don Mattingly, you've got it made!

Position

The first thing a first baseman must do when the ball is hit on the ground is get to the bag as quickly as he can. If there are no runners on base, you should be about 10 feet behind the bag and 10 feet from the baseline. The faster you are, the farther you can stand away from the bag and still make it back in time to make a play.

After you run back to the bag on a play, you must find the base, set your feet in the proper position and then turn to look for the throw. Stand directly in front of the bag. Then it is easier to move around to catch the ball.

If you are righthanded, place your right foot on the bag. (Your left foot if you are a lefty.) Put your toe in the center of the front edge of the bag. Stand straight up with your knees slightly bent, so that you are flexible and ready. Always be prepared for a bad throw. That way you are ready to move wherever you need to go.

The correct positioning for catching a throw to first base.

Making the Catch

The key now is to shift your body correctly in order to catch the ball. If the throw comes in to your left, step with your left foot toward the throw and shift your weight to that side. If it comes in to the right, move in that direc-

69

tion. If these throws are far off the mark, you have to move your foot to the farthest edge of the bag as you can, and then stretch out as far as possible. If you know you can't reach the ball, step off the bag and make sure you at least stop the throw. Don't let it get past you into the dugout or rightfield.

Timing is important. If you start stretching for the ball too early, and then you see that the throw is sailing wide or high, you might not be able to get to the ball. Practice and experience will help teach you when to get into position.

No matter who is throwing to you, there will be spin on the ball. The farther the throw, and the harder it is thrown, the more the ball will move. Get used to how your teammates throw the ball in practice. Some of them will always sink, some will sail up, and some will soar toward home or rightfield. Be ready.

When catching the ball, as in every position, you should use two hands. Your glove catches the ball, and your bare hand comes in and closes over the pocket to keep the ball in. It is not always this easy at first base, however. You might have to jump for high throws and spear them with one hand. Or you might need to dig them out of the dirt with your glove.

One thing you always have to do is *keep your eye on the ball all the way into your glove.* Almost every time a fielder drops a ball or misses it completely, it is because he took his eye off it.

The toughest throw to catch is the ball that looks as if it is going to hit the batter who is running down the baseline. Third basemen throw these kind a lot.

You might have to leave the bag to catch this kind of throw. Then you have to reach back and tag the runner after you have the ball. The first baseman has to make snap decisions on wild throws like these. Remember, the most important thing is to make sure you don't let the ball get past you. After you catch it, *then* try to make a play on the runner.

When there are runners on base, you will usually stand in a different spot. In youth leagues, you don't have to worry about the runner stealing bases, so you don't have to stay on the bag to hold him there. As you get older, though, you will need to stay next to the base to help keep the runner from taking off.

Fielding at First

As with any infielder, you must charge ground balls and bunts, and make the right plays. To do it right, you have to begin in the right fielding position. While waiting for the ball to be pitched, it's a good idea to have your glove actually touching the ground. This forces you to stay low and ready to move. Any ball that is then hit hard on the ground right at you is more easily stopped. And if the ball is coming toward you, you will waste no time getting lined up to catch it.

The toughest fielding play for a first baseman is when the ball is hit in the hole between you and second base. You will have to decide quickly whether the ball is your play or the second baseman's. If it is really a close call, *you* should go after it. If the pitcher is doing his job right, he will run to cover your base. This gives the team two

71

fielders with a chance to get to the grounder—you or the second baseman.

On sacrifice bunts, you should try to throw the ball to second base to get the lead runner out. As soon as the batter squares around to bunt, you should charge toward home and be ready to field the ball. The second baseman will cover first for you, and the shortstop will slide over to second.

When you field the bunt, again, keep your glove down, use two hands, and follow the ball with your eyes all the way into your glove. You then have a split second to decide whether to throw to second or first base.

The catcher, if he has learned correctly, will shout out advice to help you while you are fielding the ball. "Still time at second!" he might yell. But you should still learn from experience and practice what the right play will be in cases like this.

If you know you have a slow runner on first, or if the bunt got to you quickly, you will probably throw to second. If someone fast is racing toward second, don't bother. Just throw to first and get the sure out.

When you throw to second base, the ball should be fired quickly and accurately. Try to aim the ball about head height, right over the bag or slightly toward the third base side. You should also time your throw so it doesn't reach the bag before your fielder does. If the ball and baseman get there at the same time, your teammate can touch the bag quickly and then get out of the way before the runner barrels into him. Everyone will thank you for that!

If a regular ground ball is hit to you and a runner is on first, you might be able to make a double play. It is tricky, though. You must cleanly field the ball, throw to your teammate at second and then hurry to first so you can catch the relay back to you. If the ball is hit to the far right of the bag, you probably won't have time to get back to the base. Your pitcher should be there to receive the relay.

On any other ground ball hit to you with no runners on base, you have to decide whether you can beat the runner to the bag, or if you should throw to the pitcher coming over to cover first. This play also requires excellent timing and lots of practice.

Here's what to do if you decide to throw to the pitcher

A good first baseman like Don Mattingly always remembers to keep his eye on the ball until it is in his glove.

in that situation. After fielding the ball, you should run toward the pitcher, who should be racing toward first. Throw the ball so it gets to him at least two steps in front of the bag—more if possible. That way he doesn't have to worry about catching the ball and touching the bag at the same time. He can catch, then touch, and the batter is out!

When you throw the ball to the pitcher, use an underhand toss if possible. Carry the ball in front of you before you throw, so he can see it clearly. Don't throw it too hard, but make sure it will get there in time. And as you release the ball, keep running toward first. This gives the ball more speed, and helps the throw go straighter.

On pop flies, try to catch everything on the right side of the infield. Go for every pop-up midway between home and first. The ball is usually spinning toward *you*, not the catcher. If the pop-up is near the sideline fence or stands, run all the way to the wall or fence first, then look up. This is better than watching the ball the whole way, while slowly inching toward the wall. It also helps keep you from running into the wall, which could make you drop the ball or, worse, injure yourself.

Summary

Remember to work on these areas if you want to be a first baseman:

- Footwork! Shift to the left and right, and then stretch forward around the bag.
- Learn to catch all types of throws from your infielders—high, low, wide and in the dirt.

- Leave the bag to catch wild throws and then tag the runner.
- Throw to the pitcher when he covers first on grounders.
- Catch every pop fly in your area.
- Field bunts and grounders, then throw accurately to second.
- Practice the tricky first-to-second-and-back-to-first double play.
- Get used to all of your infielders' throws.

Second Base

"The Pivot Man!" If you cover second, having quick feet and good hands will be your specialties. One of the most exciting plays in baseball is the double play. The second baseman is involved in more double plays than any other player, so you know how important you are going to be.

Above everything else, a second baseman must be quick. You have a lot of ground to protect. You need quick hands for catching the ball, digging it out of your glove and relaying it to first base. And you need quick foot action, to tag the base and move out of the way when a runner is sliding towards you.

Having a strong and accurate arm is also vital. You need to throw from a lot of weird positions, sometimes with a runner cutting your legs out from under you with his slide.

You also need to be intelligent and alert about what is going on around you. The second baseman often acts as a team leader. You need to really understand the game so you can make snap decisions.

The Stance

At second base, you should start every play standing the way all fielders do. Your feet should be shoulder-width apart. Your toes should point out slightly. This makes it easier to turn and move in any direction on a ground ball.

Your hands should be on or at your knees until the ball is pitched. Then let them hang loosely at your sides. Keep your body relaxed. As the ball is pitched, most infielders like to move a step or two toward the plate. This is so their

The proper second base stance.

feet are ready for action. Your weight should be over the balls of your feet, not on your toes.

By being comfortable and staying low to the ground, you should be able to move in any direction quickly.

Position

If no runner is on base, you should play as deep in the infield as you can. This is especially true if you have a strong arm and you can quickly come in on slow grounders.

If a runner is on first, move in a few steps and play closer to the bag. If the batter is lefthanded, stand a little closer to first base. If he is also a "pull" hitter, meaning that he usually hits it down the first base line, stand a little deeper in the field.

If there is a runner on third and fewer than two outs, your coach might signal the infielders to move in closer to the plate. This way, any ground balls can be caught quickly and thrown home in time to get the out.

Fielding

The main thing to remember when you are fielding a grounder is to watch the ball all the way, stay low and move toward it. You need to stay low so the ball won't go under your glove and between your legs. If the ball starts bouncing into the air, it is easy to stop it. Keep your hands in front of your body. They should be loose and relaxed so they can "give" when the ball hits your glove.

Keep your head down until the ball is in your glove. Almost every error you make will be because you took your eyes off the ball.

The key to fielding grounders is to play the ball—don't let the ball play you. As soon as the ball is hit you should move in, judge the hops, then position yourself to catch it after it takes one more nice, easy hop.

Even short hops can be easy if you expect them. (And if you have practiced catching them.) But if you stand in one place and let the ball play you, then you wind up with funny, in-between hops that are hard to handle.

Throwing

Of course, once you have caught the ball, you have to get rid of it quickly. This next piece of advice might seem

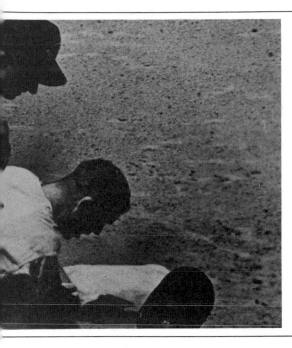

The second base-man needs to be quick in order to tag the base and move out of the way of a sliding runner.

obvious, but you would be amazed how often players forget it: Don't throw the ball until you catch it!

That sounds silly, but I see it happen in the major leagues all the time. A fielder will come in to grab the grounder and will look up to throw before he has caught the ball. He winds up with nothing.

When you're waiting for the grounder, both hands should be out in front of you. That way your glove and bare hand will give when the ball goes into your glove. You will then be ready to throw quickly.

Your grip should be across the seams at the widest part of the ball. Your fingers should be spread out, and your thumb should be under the ball. This helps keep the ball from flying the wrong way when you throw.

You won't usually have time to straighten up and make an overhand throw. A lot of your throws will be thrown sidearm or even underhand. They should be short, strong snaps of the wrist and forearm. And don't wimp out on your throw! Point your front foot right at your target, push off your back foot and follow through.

A good habit to get into during practice is to always throw towards a definite target. Don't just pick up a ball and toss it around. Focus your eyes on the head or chest of your teammate and throw right toward it.

Double Plays

A good infielder is always alert and ready for a double play. The most important thing to do is to get to the bag early so you are waiting at the base instead of running across it when the ball gets there. After catching the ball turn quickly and throw to first base.

When the runner is really bearing down on you, you have to act fast. The quickest way to make the play is to brush the bag with your foot, leap into the air to avoid his slide and then make the throw to first with a powerful wrist snap.

If the shortstop is covering the bag, you'll have to toss him the ball properly in order to make it work. Depending on where you pick up the ball, you may have to sidearm a throw, toss it underhand, or even make a backhand flip. Be sure to get the ball to him about chest high. Throw to the outside corner of the bag so he doesn't have to cross into the runner's path.

Getting the ball to second quickly is important, but

A second baseman making the cutoff.

don't rush it too much. A wild throw into leftfield won't do the team any good.

The Cutoff

Another one of your jobs is making the cutoff on a throw from the outfield. This means you play the middleman between the outfield and the infield.

On base hits to rightfield or right center, move out toward your fielder so he can get a good throw to you. If you are throwing to home, you should be in a straight line between your fielder and catcher, or on a line to third if that is the proper play.

Try to catch the ball on the glove side of your body. This makes it easier and faster to turn on your pivot foot. If you are righthanded, you should turn your body slightly to the left, catch the ball and then just step forward with your right foot when you make the throw.

On short ground balls hit into rightfield, you will probably want to go straight to the bag. Your shortstop will back you up. The rightfielder should be able to throw directly to second base without a cutoff person.

If you do get a play at second that involves tagging the runner out, remember one important thing: The runner should actually tag himself out! If you think about it, it is something we talked about when you learned about playing with soft hands. If you swipe your glove at the runner, the ball might pop out. What you want to do is simply put the glove in a direct line with the runner and let him run into it.

Fly Balls

When it comes to pop-ups and fly balls, the second baseman has a tough job. A lot of the balls you need to catch are high, twisting flys that are hard to follow. And you are covering a *huge* area. In addition to the infield in front of you, the short fly to the outfield and pop-ups behind first base are yours, too.

Whenever possible, you want the outfielders to handle the catch. That means you have to talk to them during the play. There is nothing more embarrassing or more dangerous than rushing into the outfield and having a teammate come barreling into you from behind.

On any ball you know you can catch, call for it. "I've got it! . . . I've got it!" should do the trick. If the outfielder thinks *he* can make the catch, he should call you off by yelling, "It's mine!" If you talk to each other, everything will be fine. Just remember to let everyone know where you are by yelling the whole time.

Summary

You need to do these things all the time if you want to be a good second baseman:

- Work with your shortstop as much as you can. Play catch and throw to each other as you take turns covering second.
- Spend a lot of time catching ground balls.
- Have someone hit pop flies to you. (Ryne Sandberg, the Chicago Cubs second baseman who set the all-time major league record for consecutive games without an error, says he still practices this every day!)
- Run to your left, pivot and throw. Then run to your right, pivot and throw.
- Run as much as you can to strengthen your legs. Practice stopping and starting quickly when you are warmed up.
- Squeeze a handgrip or rubber ball to strengthen your wrists and forearms.
- Charge in on slow rolling balls, scooping them up and, while still down low to the ground, throw to first.

Third Base

This is the "Hot Corner!" Stay on your toes or you will be drilled into the ground. I told you earlier I was a pitcher, and that really was the spot I loved the most. But you can't pitch every day, so my other position, the one I played for most of my baseball career, was third base. A lot of pitchers make good third basemen, since you need a strong arm to make that long throw to first.

If you could find the perfect third baseman, he would have a strong, accurate arm, sure hands and tremendous quickness and agility. I had the strong arm and sure hands. It was the lack of quickness that almost did me in now and then.

The position is known as the "hot corner" for a good reason. Righthanded power hitters, when they catch a pitch and pull it down toward third, can almost nail you to the ground before you have a chance to react. This is more of a problem in professional and college ball, but even in youth leagues you will see line drives that take real speed to handle.

I remember one ball that was hit so hard that it seemed to come at me in slow motion. I know that sounds weird, but you'll see what I mean when it happens to you. The ball was flying to me with absolutely no spin on it . . . the perfect knuckleball. A knuckleball dances around and moves in the air so much that no one knows where it's going.

That is what happened to me on that liner. I remember getting my glove up as if I was going to catch it. The next thing I remember was the ball hitting me squarely in the chest and knocking me down like a bowling pin. I didn't get any part of my glove on it. To this day, I don't know how that ball could have gotten through my hands, but I knew from then on what they mean when an announcer says, "There's a hot shot down the third base line."

When you play third, quick reactions are more important than being able to run fast. You usually don't have time to take more than one or two quick steps, and maybe a dive, to get to the ball. Bunts or slow running grounders can be tough to get to, but quickness in reacting to the ball is always more important than raw speed.

The Stance and Position

At third base, you have to set up just like all the other infielders. Your feet should be about shoulder-width apart and your knees should be slightly flexed. Your weight should be balanced evenly. Start moving when the pitcher starts his delivery. Either rock side to to side or take a step toward home. It's much easier to react to the ball when you are moving than when you are caught standing still.

Your position in the field varies with the type of batter and the situation in the game. The normal position is about four or five steps away from the foul line, and about two or three feet behind the base. If you think the batter might hit into a double play, you should stand even with the bag. Move to the edge of the infield grass (about three steps in front of the bag) if you expect a bunt or want to keep the runner on third from scoring on a grounder.

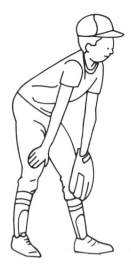

The correct third base stance.

Fielding

When fielding grounders, you want to be very low to the ground. I liked to keep my glove almost touching the ground while I waited for grounders. It's a lot easier to come up for a high bounce than it is to get down for a ground skimmer.

You should always try to field every ball with both hands. This helps keep the ball in the glove once you catch it, and it is easier to bring the ball up into a throwing position. You can start gripping the ball while you raise your glove into the air.

Get used to sliding your feet from side to side while waiting for a grounder. To keep your body square to the oncoming ball, you need to make short, quick steps as you slide into position. Of course, on hard-hit grounders you won't have time to do this.

Move in on the ball whenever possible. You can determine on what hop to catch the ball this way, instead of sitting back and letting the ball play you.

On balls hit to your right, plant your right foot and fire to first base after you make the catch. If it is a sharply hit ball, you might need to make a cross-over step. A cross-over step is when you take the foot on the opposite side of where the ball is hit (your right foot on a ball hit to your left side) and bring it in front of your body as you step toward the ball. This helps get you moving quickly. You will probably have to make a backhand catch on plays like this, then plant and throw.

The third baseman should take every grounder hit to his left that he can reach. You will have a better angle on the ball than the shortstop, and your throw to first is easier than his would be because you have the right momentum. Don't take chances, though. If you *can't* field the ball cleanly, let the shortstop make the play.

The cross-over step.

Probably the toughest play to make at third is the slow ball that is rolling right down the baseline. You have to charge in quickly, bend down, grab the ball on the run and fire a throw to the first baseman. Use two hands on the pickup. Barehanded grabs take years of practice and experience before they are worth the gamble.

Throwing

When throwing the ball, you want to use the same grip we have talked about for the other infielders: two fingers across the seams with your thumb underneath. The throw you make will depend on your fielding position. On slow rollers you might need to fire underhand. On double play balls to second, or on some bunts, you need a sidearm throw. Use your basic overhand throw when you have time to straighten up.

When there is a runner on first, you should make the play to second on any grounder you field. If there are fewer than two outs, the second baseman will try to relay to first for a double play.

If there are runners on first and second, your best play will still be the throw to second if you are trying for a double play. If you field the ball close to the bag, go ahead and step on it for the force out, and then throw to second.

If the bases are loaded and there are no outs, get the runner out at home plate first. If the catcher has time, he can then relay to first for a possible double play.

When the ball is hit to the outfield, you should almost always just cover your own base. On hits to rightfield, however, you can back up the throw to second, but don't do this if there is a runner who will go to third on the hit.

The rule on pop-ups is simple. Take anything hit on the left side of the infield unless the shortstop calls you off. Don't let the catcher take anything you can get cleanly. Flies just over the infield are yours until the leftfielder calls you off. Pops hit directly behind the third base line will usually be handled by the shortstop, because he has a better angle on the ball.

On rundown plays, when you have a runner trapped between home and third, get the ball to the catcher as soon as possible and let him work the runner back toward you.

One more thing: Talk a lot to your pitcher. Your position puts you pretty close to him. If your infield tosses the ball to each other after getting an out, usually you will end up getting the ball last. It is easy to walk over then and hand the pitcher the ball. You don't need to do it all the time, but when you think he needs to settle down, don't be afraid to say something to him. Maybe just a word of encouragement is all you have to say.

Summary

To help prepare you for third base, work on these things:

• Spend 10 to 20 minutes a day catching ground balls (with two hands). Have the balls hit or thrown to you on both your left and right side and some directly at you.

• Warm up your arm with short tosses before making the long throw to first. Then practice firing the ball over with a good overhand motion, a few sidearm throws from a bent position, and even try a few underhand shots to see if you have the arm for this difficult throw.

• Have someone hit pop flies to you.

Shortstop

"The Rifleman!" You either have a great arm now, or you will after playing shortstop for a while. You will need it! The large area of ground you have to cover and the number of responsibilities makes this one of the most challenging positions in baseball.

You need to be able to react quickly when balls are hit hard. You need the speed to run them down. And you need a strong, accurate arm to make long throws from the "hole" to first base.

Shawon Dunston of the Chicago Cubs, with his cannon arm, and Ozzie Smith of the St. Louis Cardinals, with his acrobatic fielding skills, are two of the best shortstops today. They both have all the skills you need to be great in this position.

The Stance

To get started, take your basic fielding stance, with your feet shoulder-width apart. Keep your eyes focused on the pitcher and move with him. As the pitcher starts his delivery, you should take your hands off your knees and let them hang loosely in front of you. When he makes his pitch, move forward a foot or so, just so you are moving when the ball is hit.

The Position

Your starting position is about 20 feet from second base

toward third, and about five steps in back of the baseline. This will vary with the type of batter at the plate, depending on his power and speed.

With a righthanded hitter, you will need to move closer to third. Lefthanded batters should be covered closer to second base. Batters with a lot of speed should be played a few steps closer to home plate, so you can cut down the time it will take you to get the ball and throw to first.

Fielding

Just like all infielders, you need to stay low when fielding grounders. Your glove should be almost touching the ground to make sure nothing hops under it. Remember the three golden rules of fielding:

1) Don't take your eyes off the ball until it's in your glove.

2) Field every ball you can with two hands. This is much safer and enables you to move into the throwing motion quickly and smoothly.

3) Charge the ball! Always keep coming in on the ball, because you can determine which hop to pick it up on and save time against the runner racing toward first. It might be impossible to do this for balls hit hard at you but in general, you should play the ball. Don't let it play you.

Like all positions, you will want to get directly in front of the ball to field it if possible. But there will be plenty of times you need to backhand the ball or reach out and spear it as it goes by. If you have to backhand it, punch your pivot foot, the one you will turn on, into the ground to steady yourself after making the catch.

Throwing

Where the ball is hit will determine what type of throw you need to make. At different times you will need to fire the ball overhand, flip the ball sidearm, or make an underhand toss to your second baseman. You need to practice all of these throws.

Your toughest plays will be the following:

● Slow hit balls just past the pitcher. On these you have to charge in hard and then throw on the run—a very difficult move.

● Hard hit balls, deep in the hole between short and third. You have to make a long, hard run, stop abruptly, then plant your right foot (if you're a righty) in the ground and throw back across your body to first.

● Ground balls shot straight up the middle over second base. You might have to dive for these, scramble to your feet and then make an awkward throw to first.

● Making the pivot at second on a double play with the runner trying to knock you down. Agility and leaping ability are needed there to make a good play.

You and your second baseman should spend a lot of time practicing your timing on double plays. As soon as you see a ground ball hit to him, hurry to cover second base. This will give you time to be balanced and ready before the second baseman's throw arrives.

To cover second base, run as hard as you can until you get about two or three steps from it. Then take short, choppy steps the rest of the way while you straighten up to catch the ball.

The throw should be about chest high and right over the bag. After catching it, you can make a good pivot and throw. Remember, when you throw to first base, don't be intimidated by the runner. Throw right to your first baseman. Don't try to throw around a runner, or you might wind up throwing the ball into the dugout or rightfield. It is the runner's responsibility to get out of the way or hit the dirt and slide.

When making any throw, your fingers should be well-spaced across the seams with the thumbs directly under the index finger. If your fingers are too close together, the ball might slide off to one side and curve when you throw it.

A good shortstop fields the ball and starts his throw all in one continuous movement. You always want to throw directly to the base. Try always to make a smooth delivery with a good snap of the wrist.

Tagging a Runner

Sometimes you will have to step in and tag a runner. This can happen when you are covering second on attempted steals, you are running down a runner, or the runner moving from second to third crosses your path after you have fielded a grounder. Whatever the situation, the proper procedure is very simple. Once you have caught the ball, close your glove thumb down over it and let the runner slide or run into the glove. Give slightly on impact so the ball isn't jarred out.

If the runner is sliding into second and you get a high throw from the catcher, you might need to make a sweep tag. Standing with your feet on both sides of the bag, make the catch and then quickly sweep the glove down across the runner's foot or leg and then back up again. Keep a firm grip with your thumb wrapped securely around the ball, and don't give the runner a chance to kick at the ball.

Fielding Pop-Ups

Catch every pop-up you can. For pop-ups hit in front of you, you and your third baseman share the job.

High pop-ups hit over your head are the trickiest to catch. You should back up for everything hit behind you unless an outfielder calls you off the play. If he yells "I've got it!", scoot forward and to the side so you are out of his way.

Pops hit over the third baseman's head are your responsibility, because you have a better angle to come over and reach them. Remember to try and catch all flies with two hands, with the glove up over your head to shade your eyes from the sun.

You are also the key cutoff man on balls hit to leftfield or left center. As soon as you see a ball hit there, move into position so you are on line between the outfielder and the base he will throw to. When you make the catch, you should listen for instructions from your third or second baseman about where to make the throw.

The shortstop also must back up second base on all bunt plays and ground balls to the right side of the infield. The same on flys out to the right. You also have to cover third if the third baseman charges in on a bunt or is involved in a rundown with the catcher.

Summary

Here are some practice tips and reminders of all the things a shortstop has to work on:

- Practice as much as possible with your second baseman, playing catch and executing double plays.
- Field as many grounders as you can.
- Work on running in on slow rollers and firing to first base on the run.
- Have someone hit balls sharply to your right and left so you learn how to react quickly to them.
- Catch lots of pop flies.
- Do a lot of running to strengthen your legs.

Chapter 5:

OUTFIELD

*O*utfielders will always make the difference between winning and losing. I remember a quote from famous New York Yankee pitcher, Lefty Gomez. He said, "I owe all my pitching success to clean living and a fast outfield!"

There probably isn't a position on the field that requires more raw speed than an outfielder. The amount of ground that he has to cover makes this his most important skill.

He also needs to be able to get a good jump on a fly ball. This means you have to instantly judge the flight path of a ball and react to it. The only way to learn this is to practice catching a lot of fly balls.

Then you should work on catching and throwing. That seems simple enough, but there are some important points to learn if you want to be a really good outfielder. To start with, you need to assume a comfortable stance out in the field. The basic ready position is: hands on knees, feet shoulder-width apart, weight evenly balanced.

You might want to lean one shoulder slightly in toward the plate—usually your glove side. Then, just like the infielders, you want to rock forward or step toward the plate as the pitch is delivered so that your body is moving and ready to react to any hit.

As soon as the ball is hit, move toward its line of flight and try to judge how far it will fly. On balls coming directly at you, it will be hard to judge the distance for a few seconds. In general, I recommend drifting back on these until you know for sure. The reason is simple: It is always better to keep the ball in front of you. You would rather be too deep than not deep enough. It's much easier to race *in* for a ball than to backpedal for it.

When you make the catch, both hands should be at eye level if possible. Use two hands on the catch so you can secure the ball and then grab it for the throw.

You will also need to stop ground balls in the outfield. Get down low, get in front of the ball and follow the ball all the way into your glove.

One of your toughest plays will be coming in hard for a sinking line drive. Because of the spin on these, they tend to sink and curve away from you. You have to be able to quickly judge whether you have a chance to get to it in time. If you guess wrong on a catch at shoestring level, the ball will skip all the way to the wall behind you. Wait an extra second on these before making a commitment. As you come in, stop as soon as you realize there is no chance of getting there. Try to take the ball on one long hop. Keep your glove down and your body in front of the ball. Make sure you block it no matter what.

Don't attempt to make a miraculous catch unless it's late in the game and the winning run is about to score. If you have to dive for the catch, stay relaxed, double up and roll as you hit the ground. Just tuck your chin and one shoulder in and roll over. This way you can bounce back up and make the throw if you catch it, or run after it if you miss.

On flies hit to your left or right, the cross-over step is your first move. If you are going to your right, bring your left leg over in front of your body and push off with your right foot. To go left, do just the opposite.

You need this quick start to make sure you reach the ball in time. When you play left or rightfield, balls hit down the baseline tend to curve even more toward the line. That is because the angle of the bat on these hits has given the ball spin, and it will make them hook as they fly through the air.

Try to keep fly balls in front of you as running forward is easier than scrambling backwards.

After taking off for the fly, race to a position to make the catch, then slam on the brakes with your outside foot. If you are going to your left, this will be your left foot. If you are going right, brake with your right foot. If you don't have time, and have to make a running catch, be sure to keep your eye on the ball until it's in your glove.

Going back for a fly ball is tricky. If it's a long fly, the only way to go back fast enough is to turn your back on it and run as fast as you can to the spot you think it is headed. But to do this, you have to have a lot of experience in judging fly balls. When you are starting out, you should turn your body at an angle and watch the flight of the ball as you run. You won't be able to get back far enough on some flies, but you will learn to judge them better for the future.

If it's a very long, high fly ball, and you're playing on a fenced field, the first thing to do is run to the fence. You never want to crash into the wall while you're running for the ball with your head up, so just concentrate first on going all the way to the fence. Then come in on the ball if it is short of the fence. This is much easier than backpedaling and not knowing where the fence is. It also keeps you from running into the wall and dropping the ball or injuring yourself.

Another troublesome area for outfielders is fighting the sun. Fly balls can easily be lost in the glare. Shield your eyes with your glove. Hold your glove up and block out the sun when the pitch is made. That way you can pick up the flight of the ball either above or below your glove and then start moving for it.

A ball hit directly into the sun can't be seen even with sunglasses. Try to play the ball from the side. Don't come at it in a direct line with the sun. It takes a lot of practice to do this right.

Communication

Outfielders need to communicate on fly balls. On balls hit between right and center or left and center, both fielders are in the play. As soon as you are sure you can make the catch, call for it. "I've got it!" is all it takes.

The other outfielder should answer, "Take it," so each player knows what the other is doing. If you don't answer when your teammate calls, he might take his eyes off the ball and look for you to make sure he doesn't run into you. That could cost him the catch.

You also need to talk to each other on long flies. Your teammate can tell you how close you are to the fence by saying, "Plenty of room," or "Few more steps." This helps you prepare for the catch without worrying about hitting the fence.

On short fly balls, you should talk to your infielders. Call them off any pop-ups that you can get to, and do it loudly. As we have discussed, it is easier to make the catch with the ball in front of you than when you are backing up, so the outfielder should take every pop-up possible.

Throwing

Throwing the ball from the outfield demands a strong and accurate arm. Remember, whenever possible, position your body so you are set to throw the ball as soon as you catch it. Get a good grip on the ball when it is in

102

Even sunglasses won't help you see a ball hit directly in the sun. Use your glove to help shield the light and try to catch the ball from the side.

your glove. Hold the ball across the seams and make an overhand delivery. This gives the ball good backspin and prevents the ball from curving sideways.

As soon as you catch the ball, shift your weight back onto your pivot foot and step with your other foot pointing in the direction of your throw. Your arm should be well away from your body so you can make a long, fluid motion. Follow through with your whole body to provide additional strength to the throw.

If you are throwing directly to a base in order to make an out, rather than using a cutoff man, make sure you throw low. Balls that are thrown too high in the air will sail and float over your target. If a throw is too low, the worst it will do is bounce to your teammate.

Summary

- Work in the infield to learn how to handle ground balls.
- Practice going after fly balls hit over your head.
- Work on judging fly balls, especially line drives.
- Be observant even when you are on the bench. See how balls come off the bat and how they move through the air.
- Practice catching flies in the sun.
- Work on throwing the ball accurately from a distance.

Whether you play leftfield, centerfield or rightfield, you always need to be ready. I know some players feel that playing the outfield is like being banished from the game. That is not true at all. Outfielders are vitally important.

Picture yourself playing rightfield. The game is in the bottom of the sixth inning. Your team is ahead 7-5. There are two outs, but the bases are loaded. If you get one more out your team wins.

Suddenly, there's a high fly ball coming out toward rightfield. Everyone on your team is yelling, "Catch it! C'mon, catch it!"

You will know then how important the outfield is. Be prepared!

Chapter 6:

TEAM

We have talked about the physical skills you need to play baseball. But that is just one part of it. Your mental attitude is just as important. Nothing has a bigger impact on a team than their spirit and ability to play *as a team*. A baseball team isn't just the nine players on the field. It is the entire roster of players. During a season, every player will be part of an important play.

Not all of your teammates will be at the same stage of skill development. Everyone grows at different rates of speed. Some 10-year-olds are bigger than some 12-year-olds. In one summer, a smaller player might grow several inches and become one of the bigger players on the team.

In baseball, size isn't that important. The smallest kid on your team might be the best hitter or the fastest runner. The biggest kid might not be able to hit or run, but he might catch well and have a great arm. There is no way to look at a young player and know if he will turn into a great ballplayer. Only time, hard work and encouragement will help give you the answer.

Some of the kids on your team might be new to the game. They may have a lot of physical ability in other sports, but will need help in learning to adjust to baseball. The important thing is to support every one of your teammates. Treat them like you would want to be treated if you were in their shoes.

If everyone encourages each other, friendships and team spirit will grow. That will often help a team find a way to win a game that they were losing.

In a high school baseball game I watched recently, the visiting team was behind 3-1 in the last inning. One batter then grounded out. A second one flew out. The game looked like it was over. But the next batter walked. The following batter scratched a little grounder down the third base line that no one could get to in time. It didn't look like much of a rally, but suddenly the visiting team felt that they had a chance of pulling it out. The home team called time and brought in their fireballing ace pitcher just to make sure nothing went wrong.

The visiting team's next batter stood up to the plate and nervously stared at the pitcher. Suddenly he heard a lot of noise coming from his dugout. He looked over and saw his entire team standing and clapping. Everyone was screaming out encouragement and cheering as loud as they could. He stepped out of the batter's box and pumped his fist at his teammates. They screamed even louder.

Everyone in the stands could tell that the advantage had switched from the pitcher to the batter. It only took one pitch to prove it. The batter hit the fastball perfectly and drove it deep over the leftfield fence for a three-run homer. He was mobbed at the plate by his teammates. The high-fives were flying everywhere.

It proved to be the game-winning blast. The home team was put out one, two, three. Later, after another round of high-fives at the end of the game, the batter said, "I got pumped up when I saw everyone cheering for me. I coulda hit it a mile!"

Team spirit and encouragement pulled that game out for a win. It can happen to you.

That brings up another point. As former New York Yankee catcher and manager Yogi Berra said, "It ain't over till it's over!" Giving up is something a good player never thinks about. No matter how hopeless things seem, there is always a chance to pull off a miracle. Sure, you might not, but you should always play with the spirit and desire to do it.

My son's baseball team was down 6-1 going into the bottom of the fifth during a game. They fought back and scored five runs to tie things up. But in the top of the sixth, the other team got four more runs to grab a 10-6 lead.

When the players came off the field, some of them were throwing their gloves into the dugout and flopping down on the bench. They looked as if they had already lost.

The coaching staff told them not to quit. When the first two batters got on base, everything changed. The team got really excited again. Before you knew it, they had scored five runs to win 11-10.

One of my old baseball coaches gave us the line that you might have already heard: "Winners never quit and quitters never win!" It's true. Sure, there will be times when it looks hopeless and you think there is no way to win. But in that case, you do just what you do when you're ahead. You play the best you can.

Concentration

If you want to get better at baseball, your mind always has to be "in" the game—no matter what the score. A ground ball to short has to be fielded properly and thrown to the proper base. It doesn't matter whether you are ahead by 10 runs or behind by 10. You still have to use the same skills, and use them right.

I used to play games by myself to help me prepare. In one, I pitched to a square on the wall that I pretended was the strike zone. I imagined that I was 5 runs behind and had to strike out 12 straight batters in order to catch up. Every pitch in the square was a strike. Anything outside the square was a ball.

I could actually feel the pressure when I got the count up to three balls and two strikes. When I got through the first seven or eight batters, it seemed like the square started getting smaller and smaller. But a lot of times I'd do it. I would strike out 12 in a row and really feel like I had won a game. These little "games" helped prepared me for facing real opponents in real situations. Try it. You'll see.

Everyone knows certain players who seem to perform better in pressure situations. Will Clark in the 1989 National League playoff series comes to mind. We used to call these guys "tough in the clutch."

On the other side, unfortunately, are those players who never seem to do well in tough situations. The pressure obviously affects their performance. The reason for this is simple: Attitude!

If you go up to the plate worried that the pitcher will strike you out, he probably will. But the clutch hitter goes to the plate *expecting* to do well. How does he do that? By staying relaxed and concentrating.

By concentrating on what you are doing, you can remove tension and fear from your mind and replace them with confidence. And with confidence and practice, you will be an awesome ballplayer!

Summary

These are the best mental qualities to bring with you to the game of baseball:

- Listen and learn from your coaches.
- Support your teammates and help them whenever you can.
- Be a confident, hard-working team player.
- Bring a spirit of competition and desire to win to every game and practice, but don't be a poor sport if you lose.
- Be willing to make sacrifices for the team.

I started playing catch with a ball and glove when I was about five years old. My first Little League season started when I was seven. Babe Ruth League and then high school ball took me up to age 18. City League baseball and then softball has kept me playing now that I'm almost 40. And there's no end in sight.

It's hard to say what is the most fun part about baseball. Playing is great. But the friendships with your teammates, and talking about the game before and after, can be just as good.

Once you get involved with baseball, you will find something about it that will keep you hooked for a lifetime. Remember—play ball and have fun!

APPENDIX

THE GAME OF BASEBALL

Baseball is a game made up of two teams of nine players each. Four bases are laid out on a playing field in a square or "diamond." The actual dimensions of the field vary depending on the age group of the players.

One team takes the field in various defensive positions. The diagram below shows the layout of the field and positioning of the players.

The other team sends its players to home plate one at a time, and they attempt to get base hits and advance the runners around first, second, and third base to home plate, which is how they score runs.

The game begins with the defensive team's pitcher throwing the baseball toward home plate. Pitches that cross over the plate between the batter's knees and his chest are called strikes. Pitches that are too high or low, or not over the plate, are called balls. There is an umpire behind the plate who judges whether a pitch is a strike or a ball.

If a batter gets four balls thrown to him before three strikes, he is allowed to go to first base. This is called a walk. If he gets three strikes before four balls, he is out. This is called a strikeout. That means his turn at bat is over.

You're Out!

Usually the batter will swing and try to hit some of these pitches. If he swings and misses any pitch, whether it is a ball or a strike, that counts as a strike. Any ball that is hit into the air and caught by the other team before it hits the ground is an out. A ground ball (a ball that bounces at least once on the ground) hit in fair territory that is fielded and thrown to first before the batter can run to that base is also an out. Ground balls hit into foul territory are counted as strikes, with one exception. If the batter already has two strikes against him, a foul ball does not count as the third strike. He keeps hitting until he gets another strike, or gets to walk to first.

When there are runners on the bases, either from hits or walks, there are more ways for the defensive team to get the other team out. On ground balls, you can throw to the base that the runner is running toward. If the baseman touches the bag with the ball in his glove, before the runner gets there, it is a "force out."

Here's an example: There is a runner on first. He is forced to run to second base on a ground ball when the next batter makes a hit. The batter always has dibs on first base. It is *his* base if he makes a hit.

If there are runners on first and second, both runners are forced forward. If the bases are loaded (a runner on every base), all runners are forced forward.

In any of the above situations, the ball can be thrown to every base that a runner is being forced to run to. If the throw beats the advancing runner, he is out. This is how you can sometimes make a "double play" (getting two men out on one hit ball). Sometimes, though not very often, you can even make a "triple play," if your infielders are fast enough.

Here's how a double play works. Let's say a runner reaches first base. The next batter bounces a ball to the shortstop. The shortstop flips the ball to the second baseman. The baseman touches the bag and then throws to first, beating the batter who is racing toward the bag. Boom! Two outs! It is the pitcher's favorite play!

If there is a runner who is not being forced to run to the next base, but is trying to advance anyway, you need to tag him with the ball before he reaches the base. For example, there is a runner on second with no one on first. He decides to run for third as soon as the ball is hit. If the ball is hit or thrown to the third baseman, he must tag the runner out with it.

On fly balls with runners on base, if the catch is made the runners have to return to the base they came from and "tag up" (touch the base) before they can run. (They shouldn't run if they don't think they can make it to the next bag in time.) If the fly ball is caught in the air and then thrown to the base the runner has left, the runner is "doubled off" if the ball gets there before he can tag up. That's an out, too.

Safe!

When a batter hits a ball and is able to reach first base safely, without making an out, it is called a single. Dou-

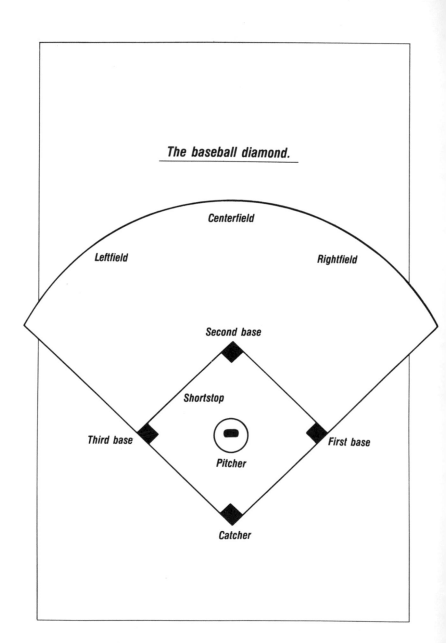

The baseball diamond.

Centerfield

Leftfield

Rightfield

Second base

Shortstop

Third base

First base

Pitcher

Catcher

bles are hits that get him to second base, and triples get him to third base. When a batter hits a ball over the outfield fence in fair territory, it is a home run. It is also possible to hit an inside-the-park home run, which means the runner gets around all the bases before the fielders can get the ball in to home plate. This doesn't happen very often in the Major League.

One of the great moments in a batter's life is when he is at the plate with bases loaded and hits a home run. This is called a grand slam! All three of the runners already on base score, and so does the batter. Four runs on one hit! It is one of baseball's most exciting plays.

The offense (the team that is batting) continues to bat until three players are called out. The teams then change positions. The team that was batting "takes the field" and is now the defensive team. When each team has had three outs, it is called an inning.

The team that scores the most runs during the nine innings played wins. (If you play a youth league game, you probably play six innings.) If the score is tied at the end of "regulation play," most teams play extra innings until a winner is decided.

GLOSSARY

At bat: an official turn at the plate

Ball: a pitch thrown outside the strike zone

Base on balls: four balls pitched outside the strike zone (also known as a "walk"); batter advances to first base

Batter's box: the rectangular areas to the left and right of home plate where batters must stand while batting

Batting order: the official order in which players come to bat

Breaking ball: any pitch that veers from the straight and natural path (including the slider, sinker, knuckleball, screwball and curveball)

Bullpen: an area off the playing field where relief pitchers warm up

Bunt: a soft hit resulting from the batter simply holding the bat out and letting the ball hit it, rather than from swinging the bat

Catcher's box: the rectangular area behind home plate where the catcher must be until a pitch is delivered

Catcher's signal: the sign a catcher flashes to the pitcher with his fingers to indicate the type of pitch the catcher wants the pitcher to throw

Change-up: a pitch thrown at a slower than normal speed, in an effort to throw off the batter's timing; the pitch is thrown with the same motion used for a fastball

Clutch hitter: a player known to be able to come through with a hit in a critical situation, such as when a runner is in scoring position

Curveball: a pitch thrown by a righthander that breaks down and to the left, or a pitch thrown by a lefthander that breaks down and to the right

Cutoff: a ball, generally thrown by an outfielder, that is intercepted by an infielder who then relays the ball to home plate or another base

Cutoff man: the player who makes the cutoff, generally the shortstop or second baseman

Double: a hit in which the batter reaches second base safely

Double play: a single defensive play that results in two outs

Dugout: the area where players sit when they are not at bat, on base, or playing in the field

Earned run: a run scored without any errors, passed balls, obstructions or interferences

Earned run average (ERA): a pitching statistic determined by multiplying the number of earned runs a pitcher has given up by nine, and then dividing by the number of innings pitched; it is one measure of a pitcher's effectiveness

Error: a field misplay or wild throw that allows the batter to reach base or a runner to advance a base

Extra-base hit: a double, triple or home run

Fastball: a powerful overhand pitch thrown at top speed

Fielder's choice: when a defensive player fields a hit and decides to throw out a base runner instead of a batter; the batter is not given credit for a base hit, though he is charged with a turn at bat

Force-out: a play in which a fielder who has the ball gets a runner out by beating the runner to the base and tagging

119

the bag with his foot; forces apply only when a runner is required to run to that next base (for example, a runner on first can always be forced out at second on a ground ball hit)

Forkball: a pitch that breaks on a downward path as it approaches the plate; it is gripped between the thumb and the first and middle fingers, like a two-pronged fork

Foul ball: a batted ball that lands outside the foul lines before reaching first or third base, or one that first touches the ground in foul territory beyond first or third base

Full count: when there are three balls and two strikes on the batter

Grand slam: a home run hit with the bases loaded

Ground ball: a hit that rolls or bounces along the ground

Home run: a four-base hit

Infield: the section of the field where the catcher, pitcher, first baseman, second baseman, shortstop and third baseman stand

Inning: a segment of a baseball game in which each team bats until it makes three outs; there are nine innings in a regulation game

Knuckleball: a pitch that is thrown by gripping the ball with the fingernails or first knuckles of the throwing hand; it has very little spin, and may break in any direction

Lead: the distance a runner stands away from the base

Lead-off: the first player in the official batting order, usually a strong hitter with the ability to steal bases

Line drive: a hard hit ball that travels parallel to the ground rather than arching like a fly ball

Lineup: same as the batting order

Mound: the raised area where the pitcher stands to pitch; the pitcher's rubber is set in the top of the mound, 60 feet and 6 inches from the plate

On-deck circle: the area in foul territory where the next batter stands or kneels as he waits to hit

Opposite field: the part of the field opposite the side of the plate from which a batter hits; leftfield is the opposite field for a lefthanded batter, rightfield for a righthanded batter

Outfield: the area of the field beyond the infield, where the centerfielder, leftfielder and rightfielder stand

Passed ball: a pitch that gets past the catcher that he should have caught or blocked

Pickoff: a sudden throw by the pitcher or catcher to an infielder in an effort to force out a runner who is off base

Pinch hitter: a batter who substitutes for the scheduled batter in the official lineup

Pinch runner: a runner who substitutes for a runner already occupying a base

Pop-up: a high-arching fly ball

Power hitter: a batter capable of hitting numerous home runs

Pull hitter: a righthanded batter who hits mostly to leftfield, or a lefthanded batter who hits mostly to rightfield

Relay man: same as a cutoff man

Relief pitcher: a pitcher who enters the game in place of a previous pitcher

Runs batted in (RBI): a statistic that credits a batter for driving in a run with a hit, a sacrifice, a base on balls, or by being hit with a pitch

Rundown: a play in which a runner is caught between two fielders and is tagged out

Sacrifice: a bunt that advances a base runner at the expense of the batter who is thrown out at first base

Sacrifice fly: a fly to the outfield that gives a base runner time to score after the ball is caught

Screwball: a pitch that breaks in the opposite direction of a curveball; thrown by a righthander, it will break in on a right-handed batter; thrown by a lefthander, it will break in on a lefthanded batter

Shutout: a game in which the losing team does not score

Sidearm: a throw delivered neither overhand nor underhand, but with the arm at the side of the body and somewhat from the hip

Single: a hit in which the batter reaches first base safely

Sinker: a fast pitch that drops sharply as it nears the plate; it is delivered with a downward movement and an inward roll of the wrist

Slide: a dive, either headfirst or feetfirst, toward a base

Slider: a pitch that looks like a fastball, but breaks sharply as it crosses the plate

Snap throw: a quick, short throw made with a snap of the wrist

Squeeze play: a play in which the batter bunts to try to drive in a runner from third

Stretch position: the motion a pitcher uses with men on base; it is a two-part motion interrupted by a pause that is used to keep runners from taking big leads

Strike: a pitch thrown in the strike zone that the batter lets pass, or a pitch the batter swings at and misses, or fouls off with less than two strikes

Strikeout: when a batter is retired (gotten out) on three strikes

Strike zone: The area above home plate between a batter's knees and armpits

Switch-hitter: a batter who can hit both righthanded and lefthanded

Tag: to retire a runner by touching him with the ball or with a glove holding the ball

Triple: a hit in which the batter reaches third base safely

Triple play: a single play in which three men are retired

Umpire: an impartial judge responsible for all rulings during the playing of a game

Wild pitch: a pitch so far out of the strike zone that the catcher can't stop it, which allows runners to advance a base